Charting the Ch...

Christmas Collection

 Six Charts for Small Jazz Groups

Flexible Instrumentation

12 Transcribed Solos

12 Suggested Solos

54 Play-Along Tracks

Books Available for: C, B♭, E♭, F, Bass Clef, Tuba, Piano, Guitar/Vibes, Bass, Drums, Score

© 2017 HXmusic LLC. Produced by Ryan Fraley.

PO Box 206
8206 Rockville Road
Indianapolis, IN 46214
www.ryanfraley.com

704438 463504

Drums Book | HX103DR | $10.95 US

Table of Contents

Range Guide

Two versions of **Part 2** are included in each wind book to provide more instrumentation options.
Optional Tuba book doubles Bass. Mallets play from Guitar / Vibes book.

* These parts may be in a different octave than recorded. If possible, avoid them in an ensemble setting.

= Best choice for balance and comfortable ranges.

Drums

UP ON THE HOUSETOP

arranged by
Ryan Fraley
(ASCAP)

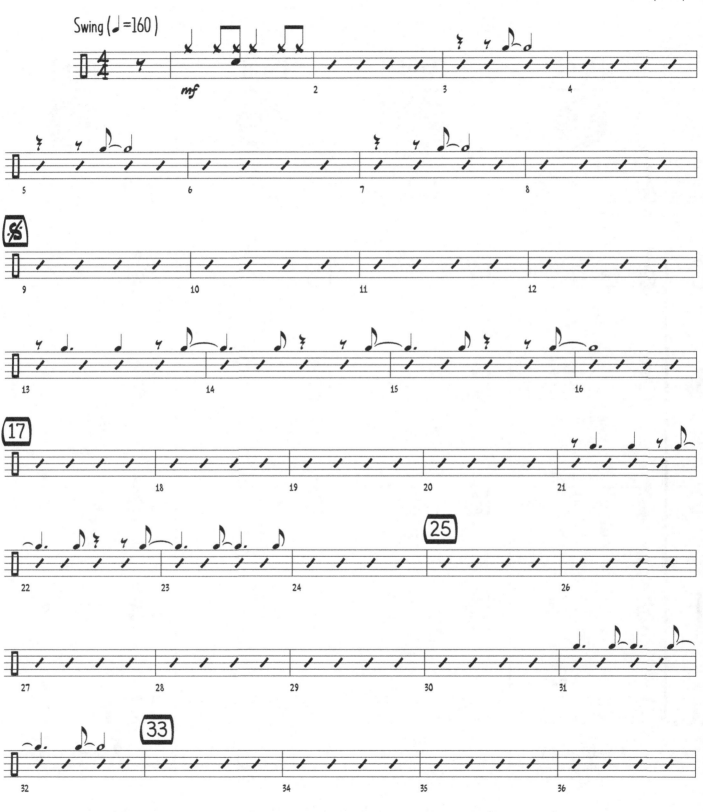

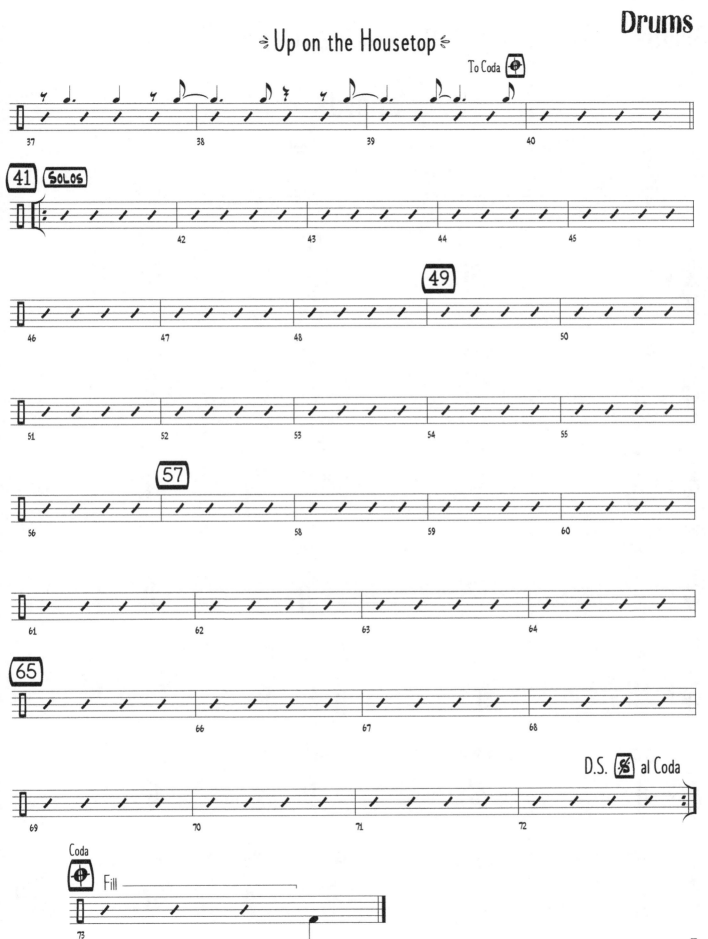

Up on the Housetop

Drums

Chords

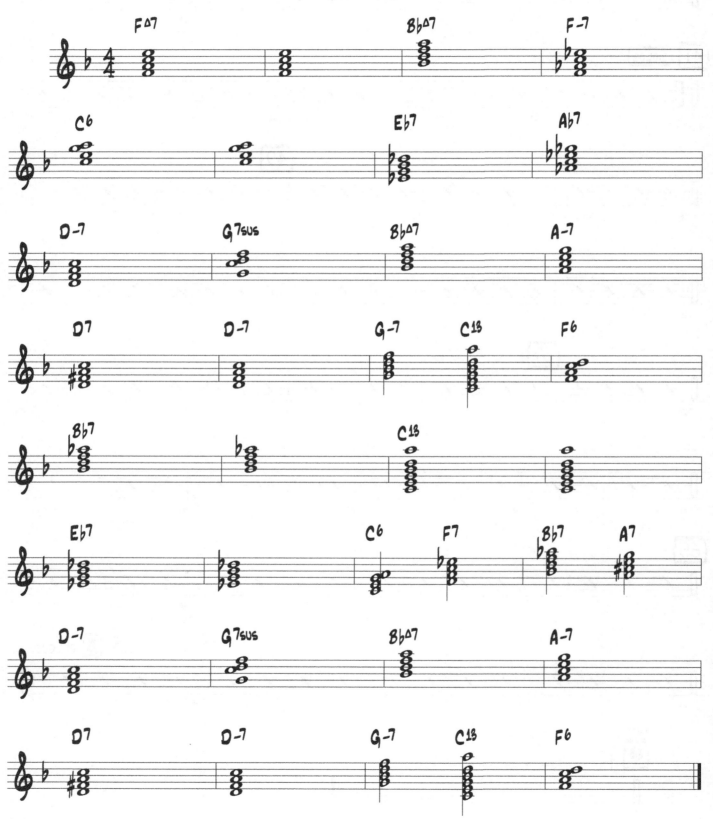

⇒ Up on the Housetop ⇐
Scale Etude

Drums

Up on the Housetop
Solo Transcription
as played by Sandy Williams (Guitar)

Up on the Housetop
Suggested Solo

based on Sandy Williams's solo (Guitar)

Drums

Up on the Housetop
Solo Transcription

as played by Ryan Fraley (Trombone)

Up on the Housetop
Suggested Solo
based on Ryan Fraley's solo (Trombone)

Drums
GOOD KING WENCESLAS

arranged by
Ryan Fraley
(ASCAP)

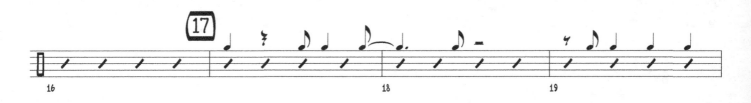

12

Good King Wenceslas

Drums

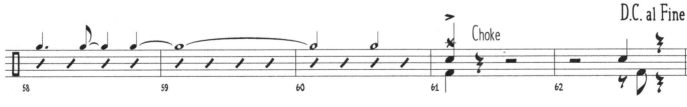

13

Drums

Chords

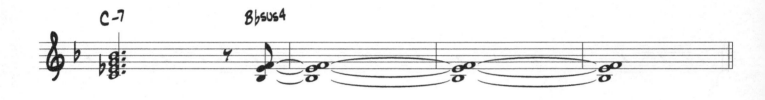

14

⇜ Good King Wenceslas ⇝

Scale Etude

Drums

Good King Wenceslas
Solo Transcription

as played by Bobby Kokinos (Bass)

Good King Wenceslas
Suggested Solo

based on Bobby Kokinos's solo (Bass)

Drums

⌇ Good King Wenceslas ⌇
Solo Transcription

as played by Sylvain Carton (Tenor Sax)

Good King Wenceslas
Suggested Solo

based on Sylvain Carton's solo (Tenor Sax)

Drums

JINGLE BELLS

arranged by
Ryan Fraley
(ASCAP)

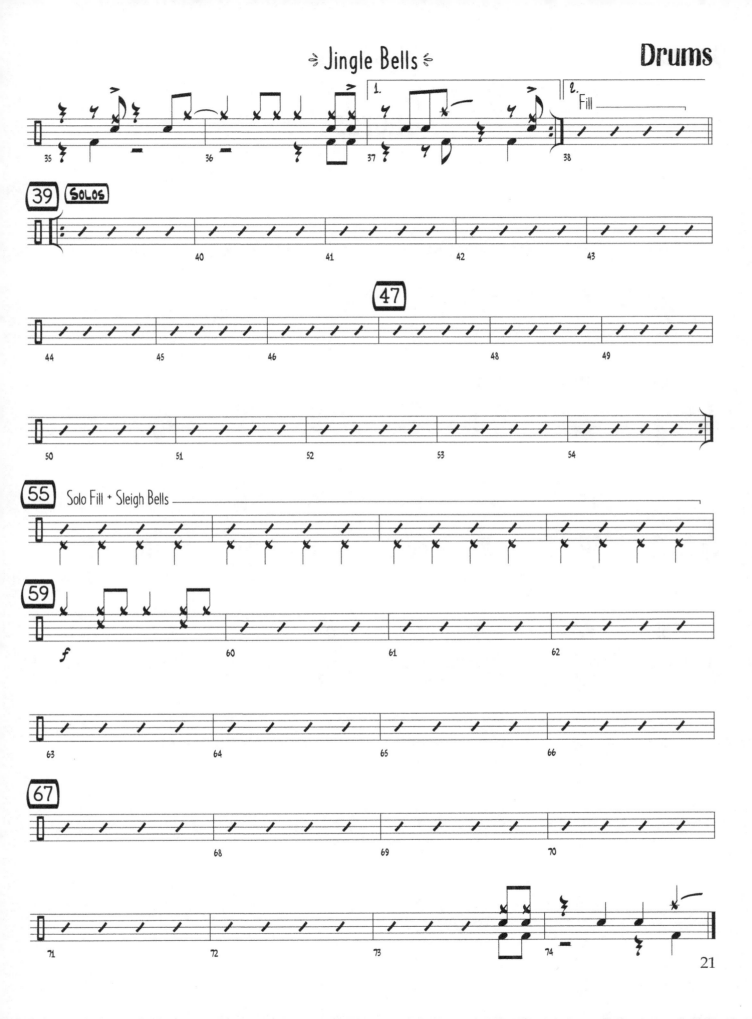

Drums

Chords

≈ Jingle Bells ≈

Scale Etude

Drums

Jingle Bells
Solo Transcription

as played by Alex Noppe (Trumpet)

❧ Jingle Bells ❧
Suggested Solo

based on Alex Noppe's solo (Trumpet)

⇝ Jingle Bells ⇜
Solo Transcription

as played by Ryan Fraley (Trombone)

❧ Jingle Bells ❧
Suggested Solo

based on Ryan Fraley's solo (Trombone)

Drums

DECK THE HALLS

arranged by
Ryan Fraley
(ASCAP)

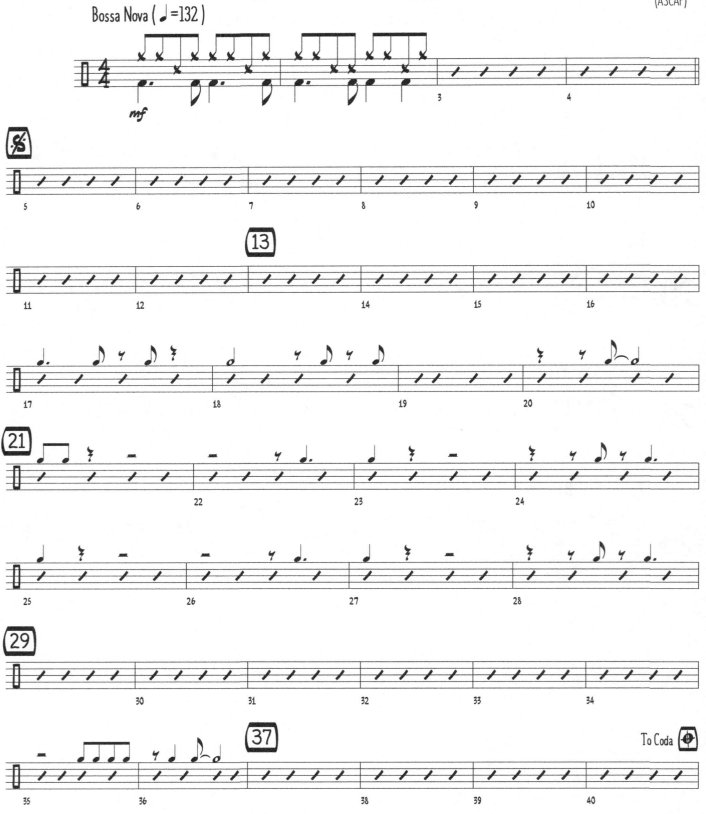

Deck the Halls

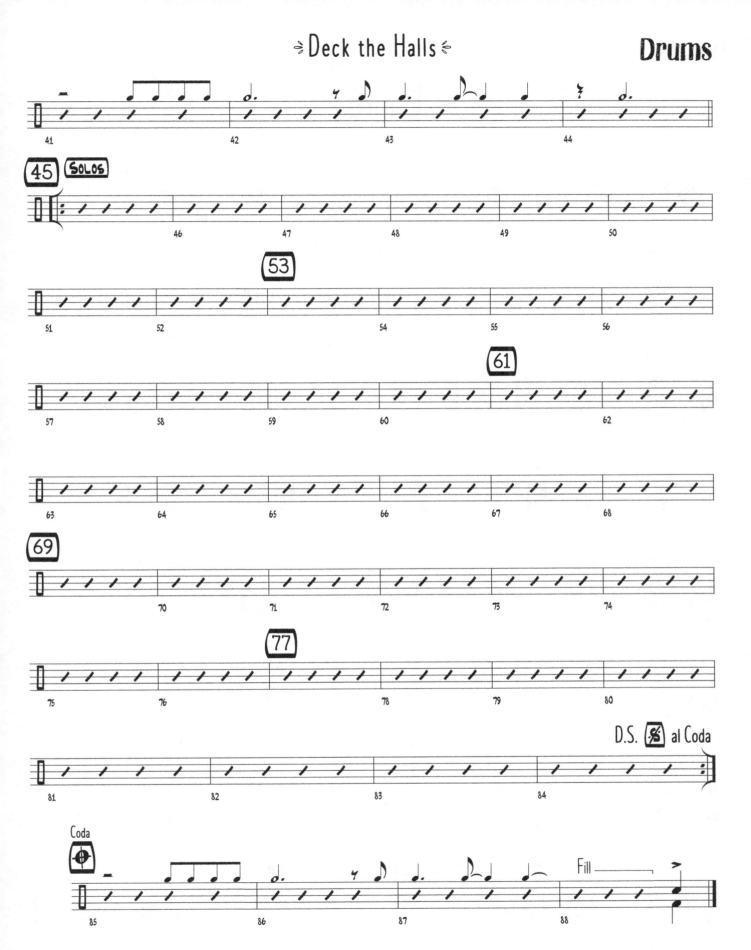

Drums

‽ Deck the Halls ‽
Chords

⊰ Deck the Halls ⊱
Scale Etude

Drums

ꞏ Deck the Halls ꞏ
Solo Transcription

as played by Sylvain Carton (Tenor Sax)

⇌ Deck the Halls ⇌

Drums

⇌ Deck the Halls ⇌
Suggested Solo
based on Sylvain Carton's solo (Tenor Sax)

34

Deck the Halls

Drums

❧ Deck the Halls ❧
Solo Transcription

as played by Alex Noppe (Flugelhorn)

Deck the Halls

Drums

Deck the Halls
Suggested Solo

based on Alex Noppe's solo (Flugelhorn)

Deck the Halls

Drums

39

Drums

THE HOLLY AND THE IVY

arranged by
Ryan Fraley
(ASCAP)

The Holly and the Ivy

 Dig In!

D.C. al Coda

Coda

Drums

Chords

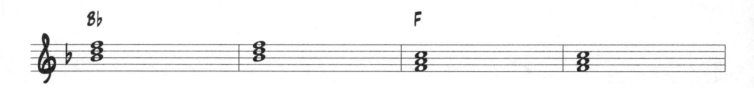

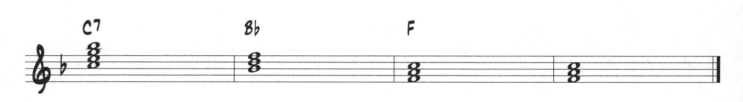

The Holly and the Ivy
Scale Etude

Drums

The Holly and the Ivy
Solo Transcription

as played by Alex Noppe (Trumpet)

❧ The Holly and the Ivy ❧
Suggested Solo

based on Alex Noppe's solo (Trumpet)

Drums

The Holly and the Ivy
Solo Transcription
as played by Sandy Williams (Guitar)

The Holly and the Ivy
Suggested Solo

based on Sandy Williams's solo (Guitar)

Drums

AULD LANG SYNE

arranged by
Ryan Fraley
(ASCAP)

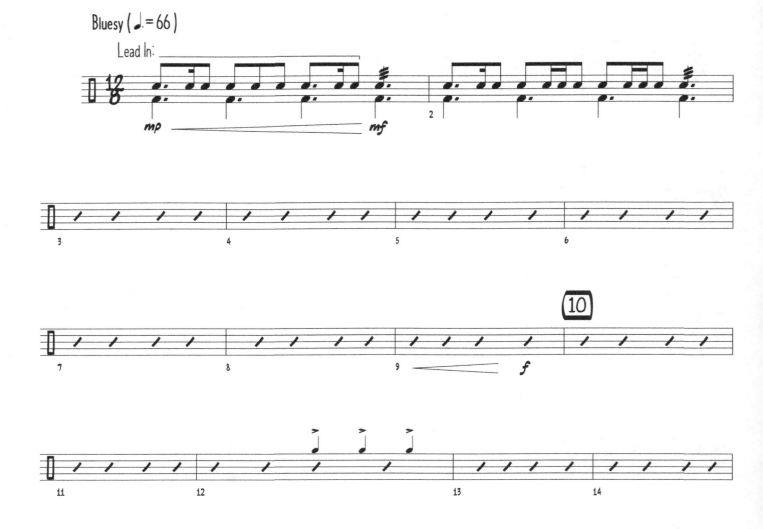

Drums

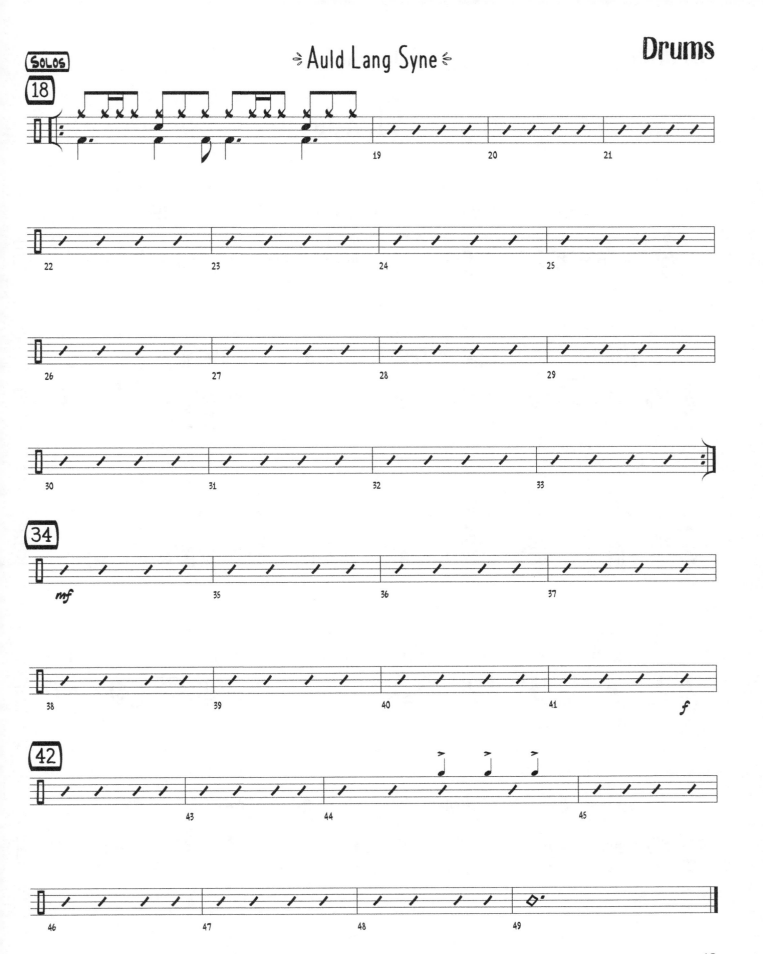

⇾ Auld Lang Syne ⇽

Chords

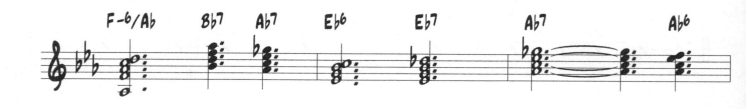

≻ Auld Lang Syne ≺

Scale Etude

Drums

Auld Lang Syne
Solo Transcription

as played by Ryan Fraley (Trombone)

⸎ Auld Lang Syne ⸎
Suggested Solo
based on Ryan Fraley's solo (Trombone)

Drums

Auld Lang Syne
Solo Transcription

as played by Sylvain Carton (Tenor Sax)

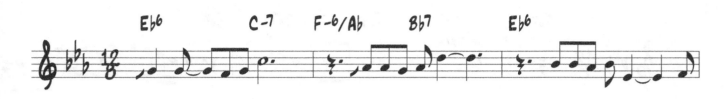

⪻ Auld Lang Syne ⪼
Suggested Solo

based on Sylvain Carton's solo (Tenor Sax)

Drums

⤙ Auld Lang Syne ⤚
Outro Solo Transcription

as played by Sylvain Carton (Tenor Sax)

Auld Lang Syne
Outro Suggested Solo

based on Sylvain Carton's solo (Tenor Sax)

About the Soloists

Originally from France, **Sylvain Carton** is a multi-instrumentalist and composer currently residing in Los Angeles. An accomplished saxophonist and guitarist, Sylvain tours and records regularly with a number of groups representing a variety of musical genres and traditions, such as Beats Antique, The Japonize Elephants, The Mitch Marcus Quintet, Aphrodesia, Space Blaster, Khi Darag, Lord Loves a Working Man, John Vanderslice, Maureen and the Mercury Five, Carolyna Picknick, and The Sylvain Carton Quartet.

As a composer, Carton writes extensively for The Japonize Elephants, an eclectic ensemble of seven to twelve musicians playing vibes, violin, bass, guitar, banjo, accordion, junk percussion, trumpet, flute, and saxophones, who like to refer to their music as cinematic old-time eastern honk orchestral music. He also writes extensively for his own jazz quartet in addition to the Mitch Marcus Quintet, the MMQ + 13 big band, Carolyna Picknick, and the 12-piece afro-funk ensemble Aphrodesia. His compositions for big band won a "Subito" grant from the American Composer's Forum. Sylvain has also composed chamber music for small orchestra, string quartet, brass quintet, saxophone quartet, solo pieces for voice, tuba, cello, guitar, saxophone, and clarinet, and has been commissioned to write music for a documentary aired on PBS, several independent films, and Oakland's 'Counterpointe' dance company.

Sylvain Carton holds a BM in Jazz Performance from the Indiana University School of Music at Bloomington, where he studied with David Baker, Eugene Rousseau, Tom Walsh, and Shirley Diamond, as well as an M.A. in music composition from UC Santa Cruz, where he co-directed the Latin American Music Ensemble.

In addition to performing and composing, Sylvain is a Vandoren Performing Artist and Artistic Advisor.

Alex Noppe is the Director of Jazz Studies and Assistant Professor of Trumpet at Boise State University. He has performed as both a classical and jazz musician with ensembles across the country, including the Charlotte Symphony, Indianapolis Chamber Orchestra, Boise Philharmonic, Hal Leonard Jazz Orchestra, and David Baker Big Band. He tours regularly with the Louis Romanos Quartet, recently performing in Hawaii, New Orleans, Salt Lake City, San Francisco, and Atlanta, and can be heard on the group's critically acclaimed release Take Me There. In addition to being a founding member, Noppe is the resident composer/arranger for the Mirari Brass Quintet, which performs numerous concerts each year to audiences across the United States.

He has appeared on stage alongside Eric Alexander, Chris Potter, David Liebman, Hank Jones, Wycliffe Gordon, the Count Basie Orchestra, Sylvia McNair, Byron Stripling, John Clayton, Leonard Slatkin, and Garrison Keillor. Noppe has degrees from Indiana University and the University of Michigan, and has composed numerous works for brass quintet and jazz ensemble. Alex Noppe is an Endorsing Artist for Bach Trumpets.

Ryan Fraley's compositions and arrangements have been performed worldwide by jazz ensembles, orchestras, and bands of all levels. He is the co-founder of Wave Mechanics Union, a studio jazz orchestra with two albums released. The most recent album, *Further to Fly*, was named by College Music Journal as one of the top 50 jazz albums of 2013, based on radio plays. Ryan has provided orchestrations for Jon Anderson (vocalist from the band Yes) for various solo projects, and is a frequent recipient of ASCAP Plus Awards. His commissioned music has appeared in films, albums, commercials, and other media.

Fraley holds a master's degree in music composition from the State University of New York at Potsdam, and a bachelor's degree in music theory and composition from Ball State University. He works extensively with publisher The FJH Music Company.

The widely accomplished guitarist **Sandy Williams** studied improvising and composition with legendary Jazz composer/theorist George Russell and obtained a Bachelor of Arts degree with majors in Jazz Studies and Ethnomusicology from Indiana University. He is on the faculty of the DePauw University School of Music and also has an impressive list of credits as a performer and recording artist.

Long a fixture of the Indianapolis music scene, Sandy has performed with groups as diverse as The Indianapolis Guitar Summit, Catch, True to Form, the Indianapolis Symphony Orchestra, and the comedy duo Bob & Tom, to name just a few.

Recording credits encompass Jazz, New Age, Gospel, Country, Classical, and Comedy with artists including Lalo Schifren, Carl Anderson, Vinx, Eddie Money, Lou Graham, Martha Reeves, Suzanne Somers, the Larry Elgart Big Band, Henry Questa, Paul Carreck, Rita Moreno, Brenda Russell, the Indianapolis Symphony Orchestra, Larry Crane, Caroline Doctorow, Ray Boltz, and Steve Earle. Recent activities include live performances with Michael Feinstein and a studio project with John Mellencamp.

Bobby Kokinos is an active electric and upright bassist in Indiana who has been playing for over 20 years. He has appeared on numerous recordings and has performed along side of some of the area's top musicians. He received a bachelor's degree from Ball State University along with a minor in music performance. Bobby can be seen performing frequently with several of Indy's top jazz and blues ensembles.

Play-Along Tracks

For each tune, there are play-along tracks available for every instrument part. In addition to the full mixes, you'll find rhythm section-only versions, and tracks that let you sit in with the band as Part 1, Part 2, Part 3, Piano/Guitar/Vibes, Bass, or Drums.

All 54 play-along tracks are discoverable on your favorite music streaming service, or directly below. Find them now at these locations.

Search for "**Charting the Course Christmas Collection**".

and more.

Or, just scan this QR Code with your smart phone to access the MP3 files directly. Stream in place or download, burn, & share if you wish.

www.ryanfraley.com

Made in the USA
Monee, IL
03 October 2023

43859409R00037